A Guide
To Increased
Hardwood Flooring
Sales - Retail

learnhardwoodflooring.com

CONTENTS

INTRODUCTION

Welcome! We believe this package will help you to develop a more profitable bottom line in your hardwood flooring sales as well as better equip your sales team gain a greater share of your local market in retail hardwood flooring.

If you are like most retail flooring companies you are likely operating with a very small percentage of the information and documentation you need to be successful.

Technical expertise and good sales management are two sides of the same coin and we have put together this package to help you with both areas of need.

With over 30 years of flooring experience as a hardwood flooring contractor, we have assembled much of our time-tested documents, forms, and handouts in this packet to save you time and money, and above all assist you in becoming more efficient and professional.

We want to take a few moments first to give you a thorough introduction to everything this retailer package is making available to you. We'll be brief, but suggest you read it, absorb it, and begin to get a vision as to how you can implement it in your business operations.

In this Introduction we will familiarize you with the various documents that are in this package to help you understand their purpose and value. In many cases the forms and handouts will have space available for you to print out, attach your name, and use as your own.

Following is a brief on the items and documents enclosed.

A Lack of Knowledge

In our experience in the floor covering industry we have found that a majority of retailers are focused on carpet, tile, and vinyl and only include hardwood to qualify as a full-service store. In keeping abreast of changes in the industry for carpet, tile, and vinyl products, hardwood becomes just an added necessity in their line of products. Unfortunately, that lends itself to a sales team that lacks much of the basic understanding of hardwood flooring that is essential in helping the consumer make wise decisions in their flooring purchases. It also leaves the retailer lacking an authoritative awareness of what should be required of the installers and subcontractors who represent them in the field.

Carpet, tile, and vinyl are all products manufactured to close tolerances in regard to color, sheen, size, patterns, etc. Hardwood flooring is different. The proper installation of hardwood requires a close scrutiny and on-site decision making to maintain a conformity to NWFA standards. Hardwood installation is also a more invasive project for the homeowner with baseboard removal, a degree of dust from the process, subfloor issues that are often not easily remedied, and a longer time on the jobsite.

These variables, along with a lack of basic understanding of hardwood flooring and how it reacts to climate changes, areas of the home, and natural limitations can become "too much" for the sales team to absorb.

Our goal is to help you connect the basic information dots from sales to estimators to onsite production people - getting everyone on the same page.

A better understanding of hardwood species, grading appearances, hardness, and stability are essential to good sales training and consumer respect. Tried and proven estimating forms and techniques are also valuable to assure all of the options are considered in the proposal and customer expectation phases.

The hardwood flooring industry has many do's and don'ts that separate "average" from "expert" and it is wise for a sales person to not only know the product, but also understand the process and expectation limits of the installers and finishers in the field.

Negative issues that arise during a hardwood project are almost always communication related.

Our experience has also taught us that efficiency in the field is a key to profitability in the office. Helping your installers and sales people improve their systems can not only enhance your bottom line, but it will also improve their production.

We also feel it is important to work diligently at keeping the customer properly informed with realistic expectations.

Site-Finished

This is hardwood flooring that comes from the mill unfinished and is installed and finished on the project site. The brief site-finished section, along with our book *The Do-It-Yourself Guide To Hardwood Flooring*, which is available on our website, will give you extensive insight to the entire process of installing and finishing hardwood flooring. The book covers subjects including hardness variations among the different species, stability differences, grading and character variations, the proper handling of materials, the acclimation requirements of hardwood products, and much more.

Solid Pre-Finished

Although there is an abundance of pre-finished products on the market, the solid pre-finished product indicates that it is one solid piece of hardwood. No layers, no composites, just solid hardwood. Our book *The Do-It-Yourself Guide To Hardwood Flooring II - Pre-finished* is available on our website (See page 66). This book covers all of the specifics mentioned above plus a few pre-finished tips to help your sales staff and installers to become more proficient.

Engineered

If you want to stay with a hardwood product but are faced with installing on cement or in a below-grade environment — or if your customer's main focus is to never see a crack in their flooring — then an engineered product may give your customer the best of all worlds. You will find good information on below grade and engineered flooring construction in the pre-finished book that is available from our website (See page 67).

Laminate

Generally a composite product for just about any use. Like engineered hardwoods laminates work well in below-grade installations and where moisture can be an issue. The downside to laminates is their inability to be refinished.

Estimating - Hardwood Flooring

A clear and concise worksheet prompts you through the process of gathering good information for your estimate. This form was developed through trial and error over many years, and will help to eliminate easily overlooked items. It also assures that you are including all charges to the customer as well as keeping everyone involved informed on all details, from estimator to the installation crew.

Estimating - Hardwood Stairways

Like the flooring estimate forms, this worksheet will walk you through the process of estimating stairways from new installation to repair and replacement needs.

You will note in the upper left area of the worksheet there are two reminder blocks - one regarding code, the other danger. This is only a reminder to have you discuss with the homeowner the probability that new hardwood flooring or new treads on the stairway may cause at least one step to be out of code with the Regional Building Department. Also a reminder that a stair makeover may also require that you remove posts, balusters, and rails - leaving the open stairway as a danger to children and homeowners during the course of the project.

Elevating your professionalism by covering all aspects of a homeowner's concerns if important in the development of a strong customer base.

Warranty Call Sheet

Warranty "call backs" are the single most costly part of your bottom line. This worksheet helps you to track where your backend costs are going and it will help you to minimize this part of your business that can quickly become a drain in both energy and profits.

Contract/Proposal Form

This provides you with a legal contract that your customers should sign and return with their deposit to assure them a place on your project schedule. The contract includes payment information with very clear terms for the project and assuring that you receive prompt payments and avoid hard-to-collect accounts receivable and collections.

Grading Handout

This is great information that will assist you in selling your product and services to a potential customer. These grading descriptions will help you keep expectations realistic and in line with the finished product.

Hardness Handout

The Hardness scale gives you reliable information that will be helpful to establish you as knowledgeable in your field. This is a great handout to help you educate your customer on the variety of hardness factors in the various species of hardwood. It will also help to alleviate unreasonable expectations.

Stability Handout

The Stability Scale is also a great tool to help the customer understand that hardness and stability don't always run parallel in hardwood products. Many who study these scales carefully will find interesting surprises that often are contrary to what they have "heard" in the marketplace. There is often a look of "are you sure" when a customer sees that walnut is softer than red oak for example.

"Your New Floors" Q&A Handout

These are valuable pages that we suggest you give to the customer when you sign the contract or your field crew arrives at the job site on the first day. We have also found that mailing it to the customer a few days prior to the start of the project can also help them understand what to expect from both your workers and the products they have purchased.

Care & Maintenance Handout

An important item to put into the hands of your customer is this informational handout that we suggest you pass along on the final day of the project as you present the balance due invoice and collect your final payment. This handout not only covers most common questions the customer might have, but it boosts their image of your professionalism with pro active follow-up materials.

Waiver of Liability

Whether your customer insists on installing new hardwood in a direction parallel to the floor joists, or you have a contractor who insists that there is no time for the proper acclimation of the hardwood - this form will make clear, in a professional way to all involved, that industry standards are not being followed. With the customer or builder's signature on this form, you are passing the liability for possible problems to those who are going against those industry guidelines. This form is worth its weight in gold.

Caution "Stop" Hangers

The most basic, yet possibly the most valuable item in this packet. This flyer professionally informs anyone attempting to access the area where a fresh coat of stain or finish has been applied to "stay out" and for how long. This helps to assure that doors and windows stay closed and dust is limited in your efforts to produce a quality product.

Sub-Contractors or Employees?

Whether you have selected to hire your own installers or made the decision to sub-contract the work, you are the boss and we advise you to insist on certain technical and ethical rules. Never forget that everyone on the project site from sales to installation and cleanup has your name attached to their work.

Tools & Needed Items List

If you are using your own employees in the field you will find this to be an extensive list of tools and materials that should always be in your the production truck or trailer. From sanders to moisture meter, from maps to a chalk line, chisel, and rags - you will refer to this list often as a check against your item inventory.

Ethics

Honest business practices are the foundation for future business. The best form of advertising will come from satisfied customers who tell their friends and acquaintances. Conversely, negative experiences, especially those related to home improvement, take on a life of their own and the word spreads quickly.

Our best advice is to set high standards for yourself and your employees or sub-contractors — then have everyone live up to them.

Professionalism

Like ethics, this is an area that requires some rigid rules for employees and owners alike. From the customer's first impression to the final walk through and time you spend going over care and maintenance issues — you are quietly assuring them that their experience with your company has been at a professional level.

It's this level of confidence that causes them to file your name and business card for their future needs. Customers want to deal with companies who know their industry, go the extra mile in service, and who look, dress, and act the part of a professional they can count on.

Customer Expectations

Some easy-to-use reminders of the importance of keeping the customer informed on what to expect along each phase of the project. The more you keep them aware of proper expectations — the less likely you will find them watching over your shoulder to make sure you are living up to their often unrealistic expectations.

—————————

Hardwood flooring is milled to various widths and depths and is separated in the production stage according to species, grade, width, and depth.

The standard width/depth for site-finished hardwood is 2-1/4" by 3/4". Up to 4-3/4" width is generally referred to as strip hardwood. Wider boards, which can range from 5" up to 12" - even on special order up to 20" is referred to as plank.

Red oak, white oak, walnut, cherry, pine, and hickory are the most plentiful and common hardwoods milled in this country.

It is standard practice that mills only ship their products to distributors and users after the hardwood is well dried. Although most mills will only ship product with a moisture content level below 6 - 9% - they have no control of the weather that product might be exposed to in shipment.

Retailers, installers, and sub-contractors should have a moisture meter in their possession and take readings when the product is delivered to their warehouse or jobsite. These readings will help to determine the amount of time that the hardwood needs to acclimate to its new environment prior to installation. It is also important that, when delivered to the job site, the hardwood be placed in the room(s) where it will be installed so that acclimation is as complete as possible. Placing the hardwood on a cement floor in a garage should never be done for any length of time.

It is also important for installers of site-finished products to use appropriate tools and techniques in the installation and finishing phase. As the retailer the customer looks to for a quality project, we recommend you monitor closely the delivery, installation and finishing process - especially the sanding and finishing phases (see Book I).

Remember - wider planks expand and contract more than the more narrow boards. It is always wise to use your moisture meter and check all of the hardwood, *and the sub-floor*, when the wood is delivered to the job site.

Job Site Appearance

Most customer's are somewhat uneasy having construction tools, equipment, and workers in their personal environment for extended periods of time. Every effort you extend to let the customer see that you are careful, deliberate, and sensitive in your invasion of their home helps to assure them that you care and respect their property and personal belongings.

We list a few tips in this section that will help you convey that kind of positive assurance to your customers.

Equipment Maintenance

These simple maintenance tips are like putting money in your pocket. Your tools and equipment are your lifeline. This is an area that requires strong policies and close supervision of employees. Set the rules and make sure they are kept. A few minutes each day can save days and dollars in the weeks and months to come.

Estimating CD - Excel

You will find a CD enclosed in your package to help you calculate a complete estimate on your office computer. The CD requires Microsoft Office Excel in order for it to operate. The steps to using the system are included in the pages of this materials binder.

The system allows you to insert your own product and labor pricing as well as your local and state tax rates. Once you have created your own store master with all prices and rates, it becomes a simple matter of inserting square footages and other numbers that make up the estimate.

Book I

The Do-It-Yourself Guide To Hardwood Flooring. Everything you need to know to install, sand, and finish hardwood flooring.

Book II

The Do-It-Yourself Guide To Hardwood Flooring II - Pre-finished. Everything you need to know to select, prep, and install pre-finished hardwood flooring.

A Final Note

Hardwood flooring is an asset for any home. The National Wood Flooring Association (NWFA) website states that "in a national survey of real estate agents, 90 percent said that houses with wood flooring sell faster and for higher prices than houses without wood floors." There is value in hardwood flooring for both consumer an retailer.

We have placed the forms that will be useful on pages without printing on the reverse side so they can be removed and used as maters for copying. A CD with all of the forms in a full 8-1/2 x 11 format can be ordered from our website (See page 67). All of the forms and documents assume that you are a retailer who is committed to the demanding standards of the hardwood flooring industry as they are stated from the NWFA. It is important to adhere strictly to those standards of technical professionalism and workplace integrity.

SITE-FINISHED

Hardwood flooring is milled to various widths and depths and is separated in the production stage according to species, grade, width, and depth.

The standard width/depth for site-finished hardwood is 2-1/4" by 3/4". Up to 4-3/4" width is generally referred to as strip hardwood. Wider boards, which can range from 5" up to 12" - even on special order up to 20" is referred to as plank.

Red oak, white oak, walnut, cherry, pine, and hickory are the most plentiful and common hardwoods milled in this country.

It is standard practice that mills only ship their products to distributors and users after the hardwood is well dried. Although most mills will only ship product with a moisture content level below 6 - 9% - they have no control of the weather that product might be exposed to in shipment.

Retailers, installers, and sub-contractors should have a moisture meter in their possession and take readings when the product is delivered to their warehouse or jobsite. These readings will help to determine the amount of time that the hardwood needs to acclimate to its new environment prior to installation. It is also important that, when delivered to the job site, the hardwood be placed in the room(s) where it will be installed so that acclimation is as complete as possible. Placing the hardwood on a cement floor in a garage should never be done for any length of time.

It is also important for installers of site-finished products to use appropriate tools and techniques in the installation and finishing phase.

SOLID PRE-FINISHED

The variables in sizing that you found under Site-finished hardwood can also be found in solid pre-finished products. The "solid" refers to hardwood that is a single milled piece, not layered.

This product often comes in both strip and plank in depths of 3/4", 5/8", 9/16", or 1/2". Of course, it is then pre-finished with a variety of stain choices and urethane finishes.

There are many advantages to both site-finished and solid pre-finished, but none more important than its potential lifetime. There is normally about 1/4" above the tongue and groove of the 3/4" and 5/8" solid pieces. A few years down the road when the urethane begins to show wear, or the homeowner decides it is time to change the color of the hardwood floors, there is plenty of hardwood for several refinishes. It is not unusual to refinish hardwood that has been in homes for more than 100 years.

Other advantages to solid pre-finished are the cleanliness of the installation and the stability of the standard hardwood nailing process. Since there is no sanding and finishing required the installation time is greatly reduced and the cleanliness factor is greatly enhanced. Although floating and glued flooring have developed into excellent methods of installation, there is a comfort in knowing there is rosin or felt paper between the hardwood and the subfloor and the long nails that reach through the tongue into the subfloor provide a great long-term stability.

Although there are a few products in the solid pre-finished lines that come with square edges that butt up tight at installation, most products currently come with a beveled or micro-beveled edge. Since there is no filler applied (as with site-finished hardwood) and there is not a contiguous coat of urethane applied over the floor in the completion phase, there are very small, natural crack lines between the strips or planks. The beveled edges help to veil those crack lines making them look more natural. It is important that potential customers be made aware of this prior to installation. Sales people must connect expectations to reality!

ENGINEERED

Engineered hardwood flooring is likely to be the most stable and normally is made in three to five layers (some manufacturers go up to seven layers) with a top layer of hardwood. The layers below the hardwood layer are usually made of plywood. These layers are glued together and layered with the grain running in opposite directions (see graphic below).

Engineered flooring thus gives you the natural look of the species selected but with more stability. Engineered hardwoods are particularly appropriate in areas where moisture, in some cases heat, can create difficulty for solid hardwoods or seasonal cracking wants to be minimized.

Combined with the engineered stability factor, the top layer of natural hardwood in these products lends itself to refinishing. Since all flooring shows wear over the years losing the natural sheen of the finish coats, refinishing becomes a welcome option to bring the floor back to its original luster and sheen. Using the sanding equipment that professional use, there is only about 1/32 of an inch removed in the refinish process.

Another advantage of engineered hardwood is in its thickness. In most cases, depending on the number of layers, the product is 5/8" or

9/16" in thickness. This might be a consideration is the homeowner wants to install over a vinyl floor or an older hardwood floor. The thickness, or height, of the new product can create issues with door swings, appliance heights, and threshold options to other connecting floors.

Engineered hardwood flooring is likely to be the most stable of all flooring with a natural hardwood surface.

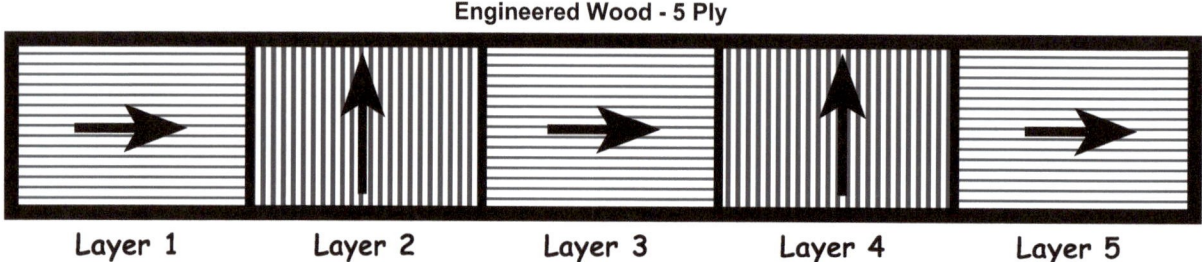

Engineered Wood - 5 Ply

| Layer 1 | Layer 2 | Layer 3 | Layer 4 | Layer 5 |

LAMINATE

Laminate flooring has become very popular in recent years. With a core of high density fibre, laminate flooring is, in basic terms, a picture of a floor.

Unlike engineered hardwoods which have a top layer of a natural wood species, the top layer of a laminate floor is a photographed layer that is designed to be very similar to the product it is duplicating. Laminate can look like tile, wood, or vinyl. ,

The product is generally very thin and comes with numerous methods for installation to include the gluing of its tongue and groove, a technically accurate snap lock system, as well as other interlocking methods that can easily be used in a floating floor installation.

Another advantage of laminate flooring is its cost. Since it has no natural hardwood in its makeup, it is a completely manufactured product and, in most cases, the least expensive of the hardwood or hardwood-like flooring products.

Installation is likely the easiest of flooring installations although the appropriate tools will be required. The ease of installation makes this very popular with many do-it-yourself homeowners.

Hardwood

Appt. Date: _____
Time: _____
Cust. Name: _____
Address: _____
City: _____
Zip: _____
Tele: _____
Tele: _____
Fax: _____
email: _____
Other: _____

Wood: _____
Width: _____
Color: _____

Sample: _____

_____ ____ X ____ = _____
_____ ____ X ____ = _____
_____ ____ X ____ = _____
_____ ____ X ____ = _____
_____ ____ X ____ = _____
_____ ____ X ____ = _____
_____ ____ X ____ = _____
_____ ____ X ____ = _____
_____ ____ X ____ = _____
_____ ____ X ____ = _____
_____ ____ X ____ = _____
_____ ____ X ____ = _____
_____ ____ X ____ = _____
_____ ____ X ____ = _____
_____ ____ X ____ = _____
_____ ____ X ____ = _____
_____ ____ X ____ = _____
_____ ____ X ____ = _____
_____ ____ X ____ = _____
_____ ____ X ____ = _____
_____ ____ X ____ = _____
_____ ____ X ____ = _____

PREP

❏ Owner does B.B.
❏ Leave Baseboards
❏ Remove Baseboards _____
❏ Remove Carpet _____
❏ Remove Hardwood _____
❏ Remove Tile _____
❏ Remove Vinyl _____
❏ Remove Stool _____
❏ Remove Pedistal _____

INSTALLATION

❏ PreFin, Install _____
❏ Install _____
❏ Nosing _____
❏ Quarter-Round _____
❏ Distressing _____
❏ Lacing _____

X-tra Wood

_____
_____
_____

VENTS

❏ Drop In - _____ _____
❏ Flush - _____ _____

FINISHING

❏ Sand & Finish _____
❏ Sealer _____
❏ Stain _____
❏ Poly _____
❏ Water Residential _____
❏ Water Commercial _____
❏ Maintenance Coat _____

RESET

❏ Reset Baseboards _____
❏ Reset Stool _____
❏ Reset Pedistal _____
❏ Re-Kick Carpet _____

❏ **Out-of-City - Time** _____

Estimate Page 1

JOBSITE CHECKLIST:

Type Job: ❏ Residential ❏ New Construction ❏ Remodel ❏ Commercial

220 v. Power ❏ Yes ❏ No Location: _____

Heat On ❏ Yes ❏ No --- ❏ Forced Air ❏ Electric ❏ Radiant ❏ Radiators

Building is constructed over ❏ Basement ❏ Crawl Space ❏ On Slab

Subfloor type ❏ Solid Boards ❏ Plywood ❏ OSB ❏ Other: _____

Moisture Reading in Subfloor ❏ _____ %

Damaged or Rotted areas in need of repair: _____

_____

ADDITIONAL NOTES:

STAIRS	STAIR NOTES:
❏ Risers _____ _____	
❏ Treads _____ _____	
❏ Skirts _____ _____	
❏ Skirt Caps _____ _____	
❏ End Caps _____ _____	
STAIR LABOR	
❏ Tread Labor _____ _____	
❏ Riser Labor _____ _____	

Estimate Page 2

Stair Worksheet Date: Time:

Customer Name:

KIND OF WOOD? _____ **COLOR:** _____

❑ Code Reminder
❑ Danger Reminder

_____ Treads _____"
_____ Treads _____"
_____ Treads _____"
_____ Treads _____"
_____ Extended _____"
_____ Extended _____"

_____ Risers _____"
_____ Risers _____"
_____ Risers _____"
_____ Risers _____"

_____ Tread Labor
_____ Tread Labor

_____ Riser Labor
_____ Riser Labor

_____ Skirts _____'
_____ Skirts _____'
_____ Skirts _____'

_____ Caps _____'
_____ Caps _____'
_____ Caps _____'

_____ End Caps

Nosing _____

Landing(s): _____
_____
_____

Rails: ❑ Remove   ❑ New
_____
_____
_____
_____
_____
❑ Re-Set

Posts ❑ Remove   ❑ New
_____
_____
_____
❑ Re-Set

Post Kits _____

Rosettes _____

Wall Brackets _____

Other:

Warranty Call

Worksheet – Appointment Date: _____ Time: _____

Customer Name: _____

Address: _____ Cty/St/Zp _____

Tele: _____ Tele: _____ Fax: _____

Directions: _____

_____

Add'l Info: _____

_____

_____

_____

_____

_____

_____

_____

_____

_____

_____

_____

_____

_____

CONTRACT / PROPOSAL

Contractor: _____**Tele:** _____

Customer : _____

Customer Address: _____

City: _____ **State:** _____ **Zip:** _____

Telephone: _____ **Email:** _____

Project Address: _____

Description of Work:

Total ———— $ _____

<u>Terms & Conditions</u>: All prices in this contract will be held for 45 days from the Contract date. Immediate return of the Contract, signed and accepted will authorize Contractor to place the customer on the project schedule and hold the quoted price. An initial deposit of _____% of the Total Contract amount is payable at least 10 days prior to the start of the project. The balance will be due upon project completion. Customer also understands that Contractor is not responsible for moving furniture or appliances to clear the project areas. Contractor is hereby authorized to complete the work as noted and quoted above.
I (customer) agree to meet the conditions and terms as stated herein.

Customer Signature: _____ Today's Date: _____

GRADING RULES

SELECT —— With some areas of sound sapwood (slightly lighter in color), this grade can also have some slight imperfections in milling, a small tight knot every 3 feet or more, pin worm holes, and burls (rounded outgrowths). Darker areas that we refer to as "character" will usually not extend the entire length of the piece.

#1 COMMON —— This flooring product will contain prominent variations in coloration and character. Generally knots will not exceed $1/2$ inch in diameter. Occasional grub worm holes and very small broken knots will be easily filled in the finishing process. Some sticker stain can be found and a variety of characteristics not seen in Select can be apparent in this popular #1 Common hardwood. Heavier streaks of coloration, occasional machine burns, and flag worm holes are also common.

#2 COMMON —— This grade is replete with character and is used in homes where contrasting appearance and character marks are desired. Larger knots, more open and broken knots, and occasional pieces with broken tongue are admitted in this grade. There will also be numerous pieces we refer to as "shorts" that average from 9 to 18 inches in length.

Additional Considerations......

MAPLE — Maple grades about 12% harder than Red Oak and is about the same in stability. The hardness of maple, for example, requires the wood to be on site, in the general area of installation, for several additional days prior to installation for proper acclimation. Even with an extended acclimation process Maple can still shrink leaving some cracking due to dry conditions.

CHERRY — Although many are surprised to know that Cherry is, on average, 26% softer than Northern Red Oak, they are equally amazed that Cherry is, on average, about 33% more stable than the oak.

WALNUT — On the Janka Hardness Scale, American Walnut grades nearly 22% softer than Northern Red Oak, but grades substantially higher in stability than the oak. Although Walnut is very strong, it is not as dent-resistant as oak. You can also expect your Walnut flooring to more readily show imperfections than many other hardwood species.

BRAZILIAN CHERRY — This beautiful wood is more than 80% harder than Red Oak and nearly 20% more stable. However, installation in drier climates often demonstrates significant movement once installed. For this reason we require the hardwood to be on site, in the area of installation, for several additional days prior to installation. Even with this acclimation process Brazilian Cherry may still shrink, leaving some cracking and separation between boards.

Hardness Comparison Scale

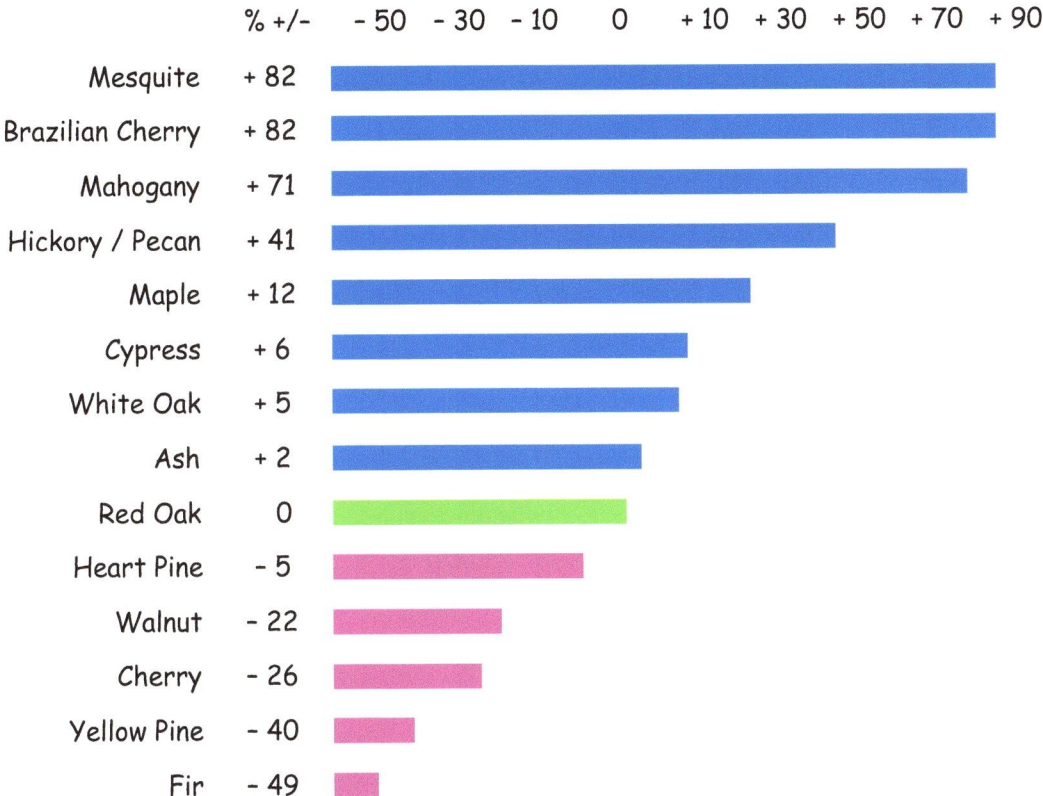

	% +/-	-50	-30	-10	0	+10	+30	+50	+70	+90
Mesquite	+ 82									
Brazilian Cherry	+ 82									
Mahogany	+ 71									
Hickory / Pecan	+ 41									
Maple	+ 12									
Cypress	+ 6									
White Oak	+ 5									
Ash	+ 2									
Red Oak	0									
Heart Pine	- 5									
Walnut	- 22									
Cherry	- 26									
Yellow Pine	- 40									
Fir	- 49									

The hardness scale above compares the hardness factor of various hardwoods with each other. The scale determines the hardness of wood in regard to the pressure it takes to dent a floor using the Janka hardness method. This is a measurement of the amount of pressure, in pounds, that it takes to embed a .444" steel ball 1/2 of its diameter into the wood.

Using Red Oak as a standard, since it is one of the most commonly used hardwoods, you will see that Cherry, for example, is 26% softer than Red Oak while Maple is 12% harder than Red Oak.

Stability Comparison Scale

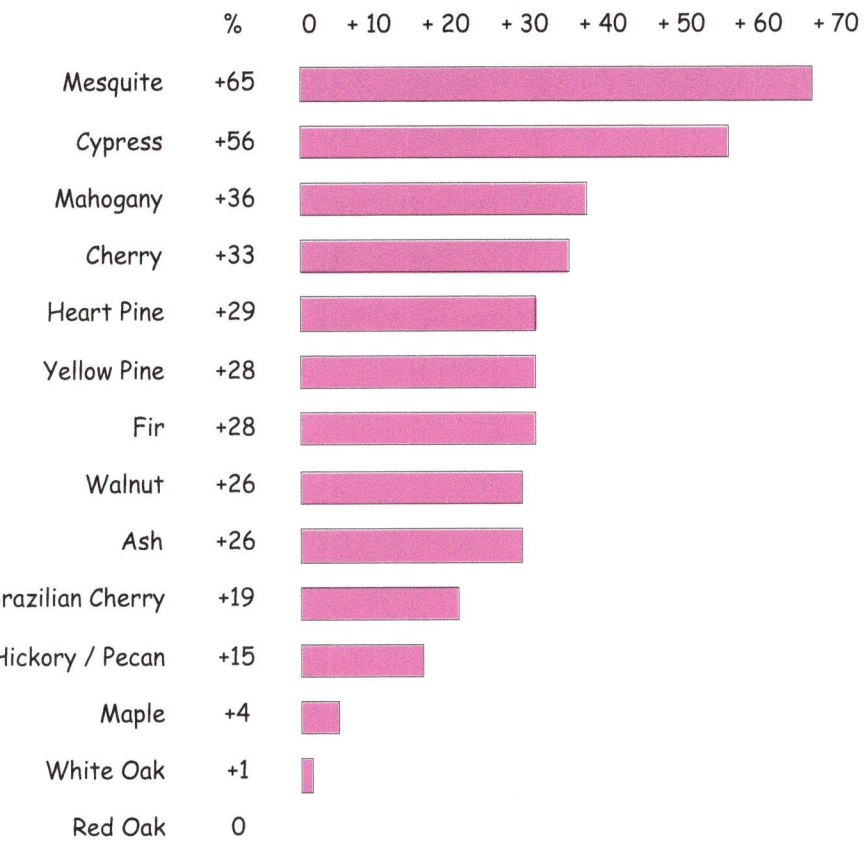

	%	0	+10	+20	+30	+40	+50	+60	+70
Mesquite	+65								
Cypress	+56								
Mahogany	+36								
Cherry	+33								
Heart Pine	+29								
Yellow Pine	+28								
Fir	+28								
Walnut	+26								
Ash	+26								
Brazilian Cherry	+19								
Hickory / Pecan	+15								
Maple	+4								
White Oak	+1								
Red Oak	0								

All woods are hygroscopic and will expand as they absorb moisture and contract when the air around the wood is dryer than the wood itself. This is a natural effect in the material itself and cannot be changed. Each species reacts differently. For example a red oak floor which was correctly installed in the middle of the summer last year, is now showing some small cracks in January or February. This is due to the typical seasonal dryness in the winter along with an average central forced air heating system which dries the air as it operates, causing cracks that might measure 10/100 of an inch. In comparison, a mesquite floor of the same width under the same conditions and heating could likely measure up to 65% less than the 10/100 of an inch or .035/100 of an inch. Neither crack is unnatural or even unsightly. That is just the way wood normally reacts to the air around it.

Notice that the oaks are at the bottom of the scale above and are thus considered less stable. However, oaks have been a staple of the flooring industry for quite some time and are considered to be a very reliable and available product.

YOUR HARDWOOD FLOORS

What should your expectations be?

Hardwood Floors are a beautiful and very low maintenance addition to your home. Hardwoods are a product of nature and are manufactured in accordance with accepted industry standards which permit a defect tolerance not to exceed 5%. National wood flooring standards and guidelines are used throughout both the installation and finishing phases of any project.

What kind of finish can you expect?

Most of our questions have to do with the finish on the floor itself. NWFA standards call for "inspection of the floor to be from a standing position with normal lighting. Glare particularly from large windows, magnifies any irregularity in the floors and should not determine acceptance. From a standing position irregularities may be present but should not be prominent."

The most common finish is the Oil Modified Polyurethane. We use only the highest quality commercial urethane on the market engineered with long lasting durability in mind. No matter how clean the floor is when we apply finish or how careful we are when we leave the house, there will be a small amount of dust in the air during, and after, the finishing process. We encourage you not to expect your floors to "feel" like your kitchen cabinets. Cabinets are stained and finished in factory settings, under carefully controlled pressures and dust-free environments. Your floor, over two periods of application and drying lies in wait for any dust particle in the air to fall upon it. We, of course, strive to keep the environment as dust-free as possible and it is also important to remember that most small and minor dust specs will "wear off" over time from normal foot traffic.

How important is humidity?

Relative humidity is the most important factor in keeping the wood in good condition. Every effort should be made to maintain a relative humidity of approximately 35 to 45 percent whenever possible – especially during the dry heating season.

The seasonal behavior of wood.

Any article made of wood will continually expand and contract with changes in relative humidity. Wood, being a hygroscopic material, when exposed to air, will dry or pick up moisture until an equilibrium is reached between the humidity and the temperature of the air. Moisture absorption causes wood to expand and moisture loss causes wood to shrink.

Generally, wood flooring is expected to expand in wetter seasons and shrink in dry seasons. During the winter months, as the temperature drops, the humidity drops. When the temperatures drop homeowners turn on their heating systems and keep doors and windows closed. This heat dries out the home and that, combined with the already low humidity levels, pulls moisture from the wood, causing the wood to shrink and causing "cracks" to appear between boards. This can be somewhat minimized by having a humidifier .

As temperature and humidity rise in the spring and summer, cracking should remedy itself. As moisture is replaced back into the air, moisture is also absorbed back into the wood. Expansion occurs and wood floors return to their original state before the winter season. It is important to remember that shrinkage is not a flaw in the wood or an installation related problem. The material is just reacting, naturally, to changes in moisture levels. Other causes for cracks in strip hardwood floors can include: 1) Foundation settlement – when outside walls or center supports settle or shift, 2) Over-drying – when hardwood is adjacent to forced air heating ducts; and 3) Improper subfloor materials – if the subfloor does not hold nails movement in the wood flooring results and cracking can occur.

The effect of sunlight on your hardwood floors.

Sunlight will have an effect on your wood floors. Both the finish and the wood itself are effected by ultra-violet rays. An oxidation process in the wood still takes place even under the hard urethane finishes. This causes the wood fiber to darken over time. This aging adds a complimentary richness to the graining - particularly on natural finish floors. As the floor ages, and is exposed to light, it darkens, and sometimes picks up a yellow or golden tone. It is not just the finish that changes color - it is the wood itself. Oil based urethane will amber over time due to the natural oils in its composition. To lessen the appearance of these effects it is necessary to keep direct sunlight to a minimum during daytime hours by using window coverings and periodically moving around area rugs, floor coverings, and any low furniture that may show obvious outlines when not moved on occasion.

When floors are damaged & in need of repair.

On occasion, damage from water leaks or household accidents can require the replacement of a number of boards in your floor. This can be done. However, it is important to recognize that hardwood, like other flooring products, has variables in grain, texture, and color – dependent upon the area of the country, even the mill, from which it comes. So – a perfect match should not be expected. Adding to that, you should expect minor variables in the stains and urethanes since finishes are produced in "batches" and "runs." In addition urethane finishes will "amber" slightly year-to-year so that a perfect wood and/or color mix is difficult when repairs are required. For this reason, when boards are replaced, it is always recommended that connecting hardwood areas be completely refinished at the time of any repair.

EASY CARE GUIDE

For Oil-Modified And Water-Based Urethane Finishes

The key to lasting beauty for your wood flooring investment is proper maintenance.

General Cleaning   Always use quality hardwood floor cleaning products – available at your local retail flooring store, hardware store, or many large grocery stores. Never wax or oil a surface finish. Your floor should be dust mopped, vacuumed or swept with a soft bristle broom as often as necessary to remove grit from the surface. Walking on dirty floors is the fastest way to damage a finish.

Sticky Spills   Wipe up spills immediately with a lightly dampened cloth. Follow with a hardwood floor cleaner.

Kitchen Areas   Since kitchen floors experience the most traffic in a home, premature wear can be prevented by placing an area rug in front of the sink, range, and refrigerator areas.

Stubborn Stains   Lightly dampen a cloth with manufacturer's recommended cleaner, or hardwood floor cleaner. Apply directly to stain. Repeat procedure as needed. Do not use petroleum based cleaner on water base finishes.

Mats   It is a good idea to place mats at all exterior entrances. These will capture much of the harmful dirt before it reaches the hardwood floor. Since urethane "ambers" slightly from UV rays it is a good idea to move mats or rugs for short periods during bright days to promote a more even color change.

Floor Protectors   Pads of soft felt or similar material should be placed on the bottoms of the legs of all furniture. A variety of these pads are available at hardware and home improvement stores.

High Heels   Keep high heels in good repair. An unprotected, damaged or splintered heel tip can dent any hardwood floor.

Urethane Finishes   Never wax a urethane finish.

Dull Finish   Urethane finishes will eventually show wear patterns. When your floor loses it's luster, it's time to recoat. A simple and dustless periodic screening and recoat can help your floor last for years to come – and it will help keep its natural lustre.

LONG TERM MAINTENANCE

For A High Quality Look & Extended Durability

Like all flooring products, your new (or refinished) hardwood floor will need occasional maintenance to keep its sheen and quality look. As you would have a good carpet cleaned, you also need to have your flooring contractor return in the years ahead and help you keep a high grade coating that will not only keep appearance at a high level, but will serve as protection to the natural wood on your floor. Based on normal wear, the following is a guideline you might follow to help keep your floor in top condition:

- **About 2 to 3 years** — with normal wear we recommend what we call a Maintenance Coat. This is a very fast and simple operation that requires only the furniture be moved from the floor. With one of our state-of-the-art machines, we do a screening of your floor. Since this is not a sanding operation it is generally dust-free - but it does level, smooth, and coarsen the top layer of urethane in preparation for a new top-coating. This screening is followed by the application of a fresh finish coat to give your floor the same look it had when it was first installed. The total job takes our crew from one hour to half-a-day depending on the size of floor area. When complete, we ask you to stay off the floor surface until the new finish coat is completely dry and hardened. Cost for this service is a very reasonable rate per square foot.

- **About 6 to 10 years** — with normal wear we recommend a Refinish for your floor. This is a longer operation than the Maintenance Coat since it includes 2 to 3 sanding phases – plus the screen & finish coats. In this service our crew will use all of our dustless sanding equipment – although nothing is totally dustless. In this process we cut through all of the urethane finish and even the layers of stain and sealer to get down to the original wood flooring. When sanding is complete, we again use a filler to fill any cracks that might have developed or gouges that may have been caused by a deep scratch or heavy object. Then in normal conditions a sealing coat, or stain, and two urethane finish coats are applied to bring the hardwood back to its original luster.

WAIVER OF LIABILITY

Contractor:

_____

Date:

_____

Customer: **Job Site Address:**

_____   _____

_____   _____

_____   _____

Contract Reference Number: _____

Date of Contract: _____

Conditions and/or subsurface structure on the above referenced job have been found to be at variance with acceptable conditions necessary to extend our usual guarantee on the hardwood flooring we have contracted to install. The condition(s) noted are:

_____

_____

_____

_____

_____

This is to advise you that we will not proceed with the installation until the condition(s) described above have been corrected, except on your specific instructions. Your signature below confirms your instructions to proceed and confirms that you assume full responsibility for defects in the completed installations and / or finished hardwood floor which may result from these conditions.

Customer/Contractor Name: _____

Signature: _____

STOP

<u>All</u> doors and windows

MUST STAY <u>TIGHTLY</u> CLOSED

until _____

(Time & Date)

The hardwood floors have been

coated with a new finish.

Opening any door will cause a draft

which will pull dust into the new finish!

Thank you

STOP

TOOL & NEEDED ITEMS LIST

Abrasives - Belts
Abrasives - Discs
Abrasives - Hand
Applicator - Brushes
Applicator - Oil
Applicator - Water
Brooms
Buffer
Chalk Line
Chisels
Chop (Circular) Saw
Compressor
Compressor Fittings
Compressor Hose
Drill
Drill Bits
Ear Plugs
Edger
Electric Plug Adapters
Electric Plug Ends - extra
Electric Tester
Electrical Tape
Extension Cords
Eye Protectors
Felt Paper
Fire Extinguisher
First Aid Kit
Glues
Hammer
Hammer (Rubber Mallet)
Jig Saw
Knee Pads
Level
Local Maps
Masking Plastic

Masking Tape (Blue)
Moisture Meter
Nail Sets
Nailer
Nails
Plastic Bags
Pliers
Pry Bar
Rags
Reciprocating Saw
Respirator
Sander
Sander Bags
Sander Cords
Scraper Blades
Scrapers
Screwdrivers
Sharpie Pen/Marker
Square
Stain
Stapler
Staples
"Stop" Warning Signs
Table Saw
Tape - Blue
Tape Measure
Trash Bags
Trowels
Urethane Finishes
Utility Knife
Vacuum
Vacuum Bags
Wood Filler
Wood Putty
Wrenches

SUB-CONTRACTORS or EMPLOYEES

The volume you develop in hardwood flooring sales will largely dictate the feasibility to employ or sub-contract for your installation and finishing.

Certainly hiring competent employees can increase your potential for greater profitability. Increased sales don't always translate to increased profits however.

Many retailers hire installers for pre-finished products but sub-contract all site finished projects that require install, sand, and finish.

Employees require adequate tools and equipment, vehicles, product inventory, insurance coverage, workers comp, and other payroll taxes. We would always advise a retailer to put a very sharp pencil to the all of the costs involved to reach profitability before taking that step.

On the other side of the coin however, are scheduling, management, and control issues that also play into success and bottom line profits.

If arrangements can be made with one or two reliable, professional sub-contractors it is normally wise to develop your business in that direction if possible.

Whether you choose to have employees or sub-contractors, you will find the following guidelines helpful in establishing a relationship of understanding and cooperation.

At the start, clearly establish the following:

❑ Fixed prices for every item and every service

❑ Rules for Ethics, Professionalism, Job-site and Worker Appearance.

❏ Customer Expectations, Tool Maintenance and Appearance and more. (See following pages)

❏ Procedure and flexibility for scheduling projects

❏ Communicating with retail management

❏ Communicating with the customer

❏ Times to start and times to finish

❏ Boundaries with customers and their home

❏ Payment for services

❏ Warranty/Call Back guidelines and time lines

PROFESSIONALISM

Professionalism is a major part of the first impression your customer will quickly observe to tell them about you and your company. Every customer wants to be assured that their decision to hire you was a good one and they can rest easy about that decision.

Listed are some basic guidelines to think about in an effort to help establish your company's image as competent and professional. Some of this professionalism should be expressed in that first telephone call.

- ∞ Deal with your customers with honesty, integrity, and openness.

- ∞ Promote your company and products without degrading your competition.

- ∞ Clean appearance is a must; company uniforms or shirts, well groomed employees, g-rated language, clean and organized company vehicles, well maintained equipment will tell your customers how you will treat their homes while on the job.

- ∞ Do not complain to your customers about your personal life or any company issues you may be experiencing.

- ∞ Do not use the customer's appliances for your own use. (i.e.: microwave oven to warm up your lunch, phone lines to make calls or the use of any of their personal equipment (stereos, TV, CD players, etc.).

- ∞ Always have plenty of attractive, professionally printed, and clean business cards available to provide to the customer.

If you choose to follow these guidelines, your company's name should never come up as neighbors are exchanging information about contractor horror stories. To the contrary, before you know it, you will probably be contacted to do additional wood floors in most of the homes on the street, if not the entire subdivision. All it requires is a little education, consideration, common sense and respect.

CUSTOMER EXPECTATIONS

If your customers know what to expect, the entire process will be far more productive and enjoyable for all involved. Never put your customer in a position where they have to keep an eye on your work because they are unsure of what needs to be done and why.

Make the time to discuss all aspects of the job with your customer as well as put some details in writing. These might include how you will secure a 220 volt electrical hookup for your sanders and other equipment. Make clear everyone's understanding about access to the home for you and any employees. This is an important issue that should be addressed early in the process - which entrance you use, is there a security code, should you park your vehicles on the street or in the driveway, etc. Make it clear to the customer who will be coming and going, when, and why. This will help them arrange their family's schedule.   Often it's in the best interest of all involved to announce your work schedule, helping them to avoid disturbance and noise. Ask if there will be children and pets in the house? If so the customer needs to understand that both need to be contained and kept away from the work area at all times and that safety concerns are important to honor.

Define what areas of the home will need to be accessible for your employees - then be certain your employees restrict themselves to those areas. Identify the electrical sources you will need to use as well as clarifying which bathroom your employees should be using during the course of the project. This will help the customer feel much more comfortable knowing where to expect you within the confines of their home. It's also a good idea to establish a common area within the home where messages can be left for one another on a daily basis.

Prepare the homeowner for every phase of the job to include; furniture moving, plastic draping and dust control, stain color selection, finish selection and any other details that need to be considered and confirmed in a timely manner.

Finally - keep the customer informed on any adjustments to the project time line to include when they can safely walk on any newly applied finishes.

Do everything you can to stay out in front of the information curve and avoid any and all "surprises" for both you and the customer.

ETHICS

Dictionary.com defines ethics as follows: that branch of philosophy dealing with values relating to human conduct, with respect to the rightness and wrongness of certain actions and to the goodness and badness of the motives and ends of such actions.

In our experience of owning a hardwood flooring business we have seen the whole range of personal ethics on parade from our employees. From the employee that would drive twenty miles to return to a customer's house to double check that he had locked all the doors, to the employee that thought taking a few pieces of a customer's expensive candy was no big deal. Of course, we also have experienced the extreme employee who made himself comfortable in the customers home by watching pay-per-view movies while on the job. It was just another added benefit. After all "those customers have too much money anyway - right?" WRONG!

Working in someone's house does involve some invasion of privacy and customers naturally are nervous about letting strangers into their homes. Keep in mind customers are putting the safety of their homes, possessions and sometimes pets and children into a relative strangers hands.

It has nothing to do with money. It does have to do with what is right and what is wrong. These are values you will either choose to use or not use in your business. Good values require a discipline on the part of both the employer and the employee. Take time to establish very clearly the rules and values that will apply to you, your business and your employees. And remember your ethics become more and more transparent to your customers and your community over a period of time.

Honest business practices will help you in the long run with word of mouth and a strong referral business, which is your least expensive and most valuable form of advertising. The more direct customer referrals you can generate in the future, the less you will have to spend on advertising and promotion. As the old saying goes - "....it is less expensive to keep a good customer than create a new one."

JOB SITE APPEARANCE

The number one concern among homeowners is the care and condition of their home and property during an ongoing project. Here are a few highlights in keeping your job site looking its best.

- ∞ Clean up as you go rather than waiting until the end of the work day or week.

- ∞ Neatness and cleanliness speaks volumes to the customer.

- ∞ Stack material efficiently to keep work areas open and free of debris.

- ∞ Put all tools and equipment where they belong for easy access. This keeps you from having to find or move them when needed and generates efficiency.

- ∞ Keep work areas, hallways, and stairs free from scrap lumber, buckets, nails, cords and other job site hazards.

- ∞ Proper job site maintenance will boost employee morale and promote safety in addition to encouraging more professional work habits.

- ∞ Rags, wood scraps, stain cans, and heavy dust are to always be considered fire hazards. Dispose of them properly and in a timely manner.

- ∞ At the end of each day walk the job site and spot check for personal trash, empty boxes, loose material, and tools. This will assure your customer that you are a conscientious professional.

EQUIPMENT MAINTENANCE

Your tools <u>are</u> your business. Hardwood flooring tools and equipment are expensive and difficult to repair on short notice. Make time in your schedule to clean and maintain them.

Dust is certainly a factor in the hardwood flooring industry, but dust inside the moving parts of your motors, bearings, wheels and other moving parts will take a heavy and costly toll over time.

It is our policy to keep one small compressor, hose and air nozzle plugged in at all times whether installing or sanding. We usually place the unit outside or in the garage area. This allows us to blow out drums, edgers, vacuums, and saws as needed. We also use it for blowing dust from our clothing and shoes to keep the customer's home as dust-free as possible.

There are some simple steps that you can take in order to keep your equipment running at peak performance.

∞ Sanding equipment should be blown out daily and completely wiped down.

∞ Floor edger's that are used daily should have their brushes changed at least twice a year as well as the oil checked regularly.

∞ Drum sanders should be routinely checked for belt wear, drum wear, and clean, smooth, and near-perfectly round wheels.

∞ Installation tools should be kept free from glue and grease areas. A quick wipe down with each use prevents unsightly and ugly blemishes.

∞ Van and efficient trailer organization not only promotes a professional image but will save valuable time on the job site.

∞ Vacuum bags need to be changed frequently in order to operate at maximum performance.

Additional Resources

For additional information about hardwood flooring, species, grades, installation, finishing, and maintenance, you can go to the following websites:

Learn About Hardwood Flooring
> http://www.learnhardwoodflooring.com/

National Wood Flooring Assocation (NWFA)
> http://www.woodfloors.org/consumer/index.aspx

National Oak Flooring Manufacturers Association (NOFMA)
> http://www.nofma.org/

TO ORDER 8-1/2 x 11 FORMS

The forms shown in this book on pages 17 through 81 can be ordered in full 8-1/2 x 11 format for a small fee. Your order will include 18 forms and documents on 33 pages.

The forms will be sent to you, by email, in a black and white PDF format.

You can print the forms in your desired quantity for company use.

To order the forms on your Pay Pal account for just $7.95 go to the website below, and click on the "Forms" page.

http://www.learnhardwoodflooring.com/

Covers....

- Selection

- Estimating

- Budgeting

- Tools & Supplies

- Preparation

- Installation

- Sanding

- Finishing

- and more!

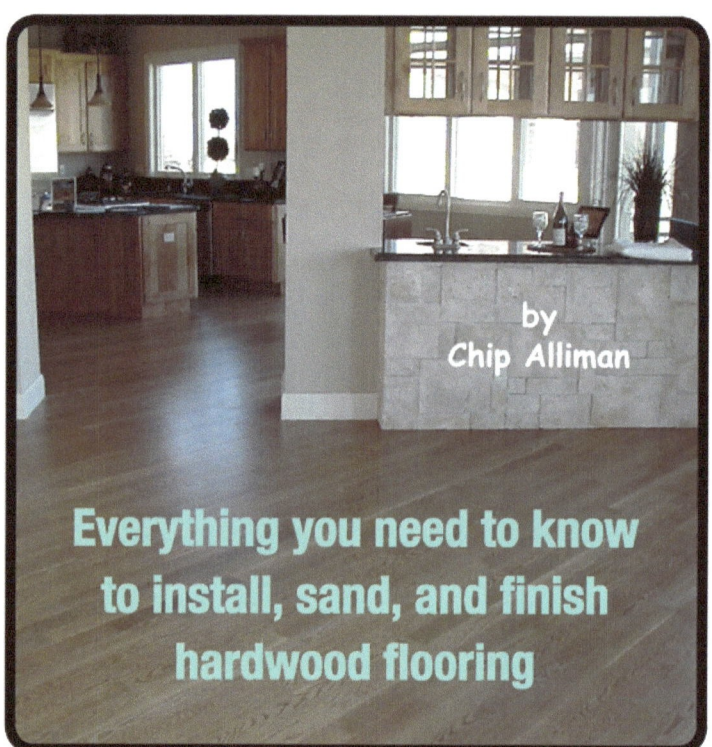

THE DO-IT-YOURSELF GUIDE TO

HARDWOOD FLOORING

by
Chip Alliman

Everything you need to know
to install, sand, and finish
hardwood flooring

This book is directed specifically at what is referred to as unfinished, site finished, or jobsite finished wood floors. You'll find an abundance of information on species, stability, hardness, and other important information about selecting the right hardwood for your home. More importantly, this book will help you better understand all of the processes involved in the installation and finishing of your hardwood flooring. We'll also give you information on the maintenance and care for the variety of wood floor finishes that are available today. And - each chapter ends with a checklist to assist you through each phase of your project.

learnhardwoodflooring.com

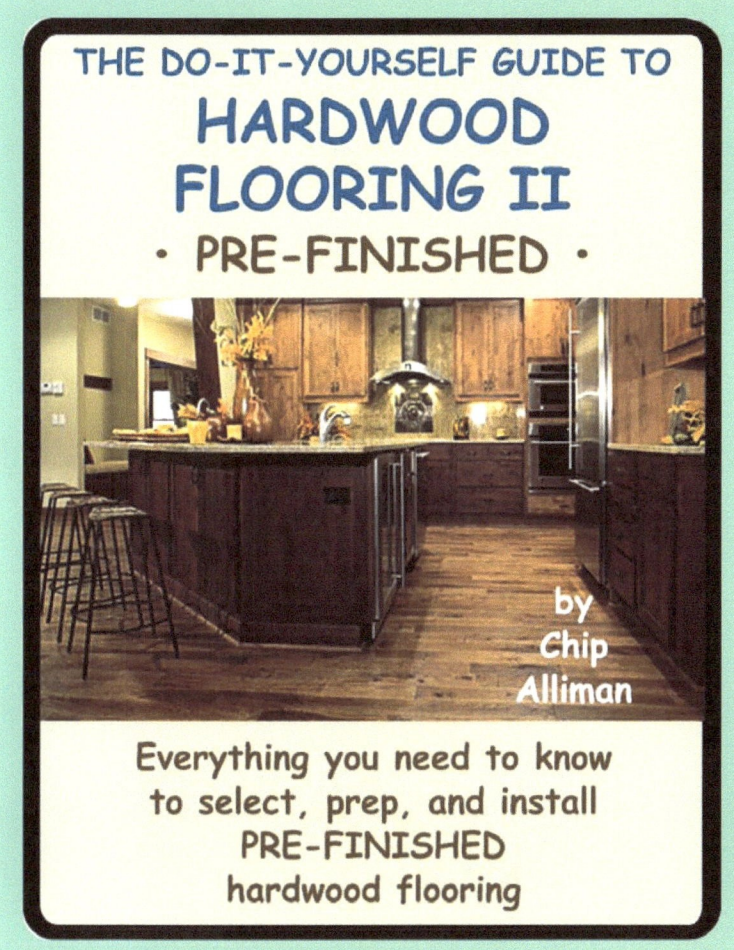

Covers....

• Selection

• Grading

• Estimating

• Budgeting

• Scheduling

• Tools & Supplies

• Preparation

• Installation

• and more!

This book is directed specifically at what is referred to as pre-finished hardwood flooring. We help you answer questions and concerns about above and below-grade installations. We'll give you a brief on the differences between laminate, engineered and solid hardwood flooring. And, we'll provide official comparison scales for hardwood stability and hardness. Plus - one of the more popular features of our books is the checklist at the end of each chapter to walk you through each phase of the planning and process of your project. There is no substitute for the experience and years behind the insights and development of this manual.

learnhardwoodflooring.com

www.ingramcontent.com/pod-product-compliance
Lightning Source LLC
Chambersburg PA
CBHW050745180526
45159CB00003B/1351